5 0664 01000870 6

PS   Barger, James
3515   Ernest Hemingway
.E37   literary giant
Z58823
1987

D1686461

9780686112457

	DATE DUE	

AUDREY COHEN COLLEGE LIBRARY
345 HUDSON STREET
NEW YORK, NY 10014

AUDREY COHEN COLLEGE LIBRARY

ERNEST HEMINGWAY

American Literary Giant

BY JAMES BARGER

B.S. Southern Illinois University

D. Steve Rahmas, *A. B., J. D., Columbia U., Editor*

Compiled with the assistance of the Research Staff of SamHar Press.

SamHar Press
Charlotteville, N.Y. 12036
A Division of Story House Corp.

1975

MacKay Library-Cranford
Union County College

Barger, James
    Ernest Hemingway, American literary giant. Charlotteville, N.Y., SamHar Press, 1975.

    28 p 22 cm. (Outstanding personalities no. 80)
    Bibliography: p. 27-28

1. Hemingway, Ernest, 1899-1961- Biography

PS3515.E37Z5823   813'.5'2 (B)

The above card has been cataloged, utilizing information received from Library of Congress pursuant to the C. I. P. (Cataloging in Print) program. Library card portrayed above is 80% of original size.

Preassigned Library of Congress Catalog Card Number: 75-33830

Copyright © 1975 Story House Corp.,

All rights reserved. Printed in the United States of America.

Reprint 1987

ERNEST HEMINGWAY

American Literary Giant

On a Sunday, July 2, 1962, the world learned without believing, that Ernest Hemingway was dead. It did not seem possible. Though there is always the shock of disbelief when someone dies suddenly and unexpectedly, there were several other reasons why Ernest Hemingway did not seem dead. First of all, it wasn't the first time that the press had reported his death. During World War II, he had been reported killed in an automobile wreck in London; that report had soon been corrected. He had not been killed, although he had been hurt rather badly. On another occasion, he had been reported killed in a plane crash in Africa; again, it was not long until a correction was printed.

But there were still more reasons why it did not seem possible that Ernest Hemingway was dead. To millions of people, he was a hero--the kind of hero who seems immortal. He was no stranger to pain or fear. In fact, he often went out of his way to encounter both. He was a public personality, just like a movie star, or a sports star, imposing his tough guy philosophy upon the world. His face was as familiar as any politician. To a great number of people, Ernest Hemingway was somehow mixed up with Gary Cooper, who was a close friend of his, and who starred in the movie version of two of his books. He had an incredible amount of courage, and took it with him, out into the windy Gulf of Mexico on a fishing boat, into all of the major wars of the early twentieth century, into the hills of Africa, and into face-to-face encounters with real bulls. This was the kind of man he was. Perhaps the manner of his death by suicide was the most unbelievable thing of all. For his books, the reasons for his fame in the first place, had preached the gospel of survival. It seemed important to his major characters, who were usually modeled upon himself, to face the world as it is, and to struggle on, no matter what the odds. This was exactly what he had done for many years. To have him die in such a manner was just impossible. It was unforgivable, especially when so many people had believed in him.

Ernest Miller Hemingway was born on July 21, 1899, in Oak Park, Illinois, the first son of Dr. Clarence Edmonds Hemingway, a physician, and Grace E. Hall Hemingway. Both parents were devoted Protestants and good citizens. Ernest's father was a great nature lover. He enjoyed all kinds of outdoor activities including hunting and fishing, and he gave his son the same passion. Just before Ernest had been born, his father and mother had purchased some lake-front property, on Walloon Lake, near Petoskey, a small town in northern Michigan. During Ernest's first year, they built a summer cottage, and the family spent their summers there in the years that followed. Ernest was fishing by the time he was three years old, and within a few years he was also an excellent hunter. He never lost his love of nature even as an old man. Ernest's mother, on the other hand, probably influenced his interest in the arts. She was a very talented singer, with a strong contralto voice that could have made her a famous opera singer, had she not decided to get married and raise a family instead. She was also a talented painter. Although she failed to make Ernest into a musician, she had a marked cultural effect on him in other ways. She was also a very strong-willed woman, and this was one trait that her son certainly inherited.

Ernest was the second of six children. His older sister, Marcelline, had been born in 1898. After Ernest, there were three more girls: Ursula, born in 1902, Madeline (probably his favorite sister, called "Sunny"), born in 1904, and Carol, born in 1911. The youngest member of the family was Ernest's only brother, Leicester, who was born on April Fools's Day in 1915. It was a large and happy family, which, though it consisted mainly of girls, was outdoorsy enough to suit young Ernest. They had few financial problems, and they always managed to get away together during the summer months, most often to their summer cottage in Michigan, which Ernest's mother had named Windemere.

The majority of his boyhood experiences have their setting there. One summer before he was ten, he fell in the woods and drove a stick into his throat. Luckily, his father was on hand to remove the stick and stop the bleeding. It was the first major accident of his life, but it was far from the last; throughout his life, he was to be plagued with all sorts of physical mishap and maladies. Many of his accidents he brought upon himself, but many were just the result of bad luck.

Possibly the most memorable experiences of his summers in northern Michigan were his visits with his father to the Ojibway Indians, who lived in an abandoned sawmill near the cottage. They were to provide several of the stories that he would later set down in the form of the Nick Adam stories.

His life in Oak Park was not unusual. He liked school and was a very good student. He played football in high school, and wrote stories and articles for the *Tabula*, the school's literary magazine. His teachers praised his writing, and encouraged him to do more. One of his favorite writers, and one whom he imitated several times, was Ring Lardner. He also took an interest in boxing while in school, an interest he would pursue for many years to come; he actually became a very good boxer, and it helped him through a few scrapes as he became older. Another interest he pursued was marksmanship, and he and some friends organized a Rifle Club. Upon graduation, although he had shown a great deal of interest in high school, Ernest resisted his parents' desire that he go to college. He had other ideas: he wanted to go to war.

Somewhat as a compromise, it was decided that he would go to work. His uncle happened to be a good friend of Henry Haskell, editor of the *Kansas City Star*. The *Star* was a very good newspaper, with a reputation for training its writers well in the craft of journalism. In October, 1917, Ernest left Oak Park by train, for Kansas City, where he was about to get his first look at the harsh realities of city life. He saw plenty, getting a firsthand look at some rather incredible things. His beat included a police station and a hospital. He learned that there was more to politics than just speeches and elections. He learned that people sometimes broke the law and got away with it. He interviewed hired killers, gamblers, and other underground characters.

His job for the *Star* educated him in another way, too. Reporters who worked for the paper soon learned that to stay in journalism, they had to write short sentences. The lesson remained with Ernest, and it continued to be a part of his style in all of his literary works.

Getting away from home made him feel independent, and it wasn't long before he was looking for a way to get into the war. His vision was too poor for him to qualify as a soldier (he had inherited his mother's eyes and not his father's, and it had always irritated him that his father was such a better shot than he was). After Ernest proved to his father that he could act very well on his own, his father began to agree that if he wanted to go to war, he should be allowed to do so. And Ernest had found a way to go: he could be an ambulance driver for the Red Cross. So, in April, 1919, just six months after he had gone to work for the *Star,* he quit and returned home to prepare to go to Europe. On May 21, 1918, he was put on the *Chicago,* a ship bound for Europe. This voyage gave him the idea for his first novel, which he never finished. It was also this journey that gave him his first look at France. He rode on a train from Bordeaux to Paris, where he stayed briefly before going on to Milan, Italy, which was near the front.

At first he found his work exciting. Although it shocked him to see so many dead people, he soon got used to the idea. Then he became bored: he was seeing the results of the action, but not the action, itself. He began to plot ways of getting to the front line. His chance came when volunteers were asked to man some emergency canteens near the front. Ernest volunteered, and while he was performing his duty, carrying chocolate and cigarettes to the soldiers, he just missed being hit directly by a mortar shell. One soldier near him was killed immediately, and another badly wounded. Ernest, too, was hurt and dazed, but he managed to pick up the wounded man and carry him out of the area; in doing so, he was hit twice in the legs by machine gun fire. After surgery, he was sent on a hospital train back to Milan to recuperate.

He spent the next three months in the hospital there, where he soon fell in love with Agnes von Kurowsky, one of the nurses. Although Agnes was very fond of this young man who gave her so much attention, Ernest was not able to persuade her to marry him. This experience formed the basis for one of his best novels, *A Farewell to Arms,* in which Agnes was the model for the heroine Catherine Barkley.

By October, 1918, Ernest was ready to return to the front; but he was not there long before he contracted a bad case of jaundice, and had to return to the hospital. He did not leave Milan again until he was mustered out of the service a few months later.

Ernest returned to the United States in January, 1919, to find himself something of a hero. Some newspapers had reported his being wounded, and he had been questioned by a reporter on the ship coming home. Back in Oak Park, he was asked to address the students about his war experiences.

In spite of his new celebrity status, it was not a happy time for the young Hemingway. After having seen so much of the world, the domestic role as the son of Oak Park Protestants did not appeal to him. Other problems made him uneasy as well. He was probably a bit lonely for Agnes. His wound tormented him at times. And he was plagued by a peculiar kind of insomnia, brought on by the war, in which he often could not sleep without a light on. The chief problem, however, was his restlessness: he longed to be on his own again, preferably as a writer. He did some writing, and sent it to various magazines without any success; this added to his disappointment.

In the winter of 1919, however, through the introduction of a friend, he was given another job with a newspaper, the *Toronto Star.* It was a free-lance position which did not pay well, but it gave him a chance to reassert his independence from his family. His parents had been unhappy for some time with his restlessness, and especially with the fact that he was becoming something of a freeloader, borrowing money with no apparent intention of paying it back.

Ernest had been spending much time with an old friend, Bill Smith, at Horton's Bay, Michigan, which was not far from Windemere. Bill arranged for Ernest to move to Chicago in 1920, and live with his brother, Y.K. Smith, until he could find a job. This pleased Ernest very much, because Y.K. Smith was something of an intellectual, and knew many interesting people; indeed, it was through Y.K. Smith that Ernest made two of the most important acquaintances of his life: the first was Hadley Richardson, a girl from St. Louis, who was to become his first wife; the other was Sherwood Anderson, a friend and neighbor, and a very famous author. Anderson had written *Winesburg, Ohio*, a book which had won him the respect of the literary world. Anderson was also known to help young writers along, and he was more than happy to recommend Ernest to his literary friends. It was Anderson who suggested that Ernest go to Paris.

Ernest had found a job, but it did not please him very much. He was writing for a magazine called the *Cooperative Commonwealth* and writing an occasional article for the *Toronto Star*. After his marriage to Hadley on September 3, 1921, he found that he could not support a wife and eat very well on his meager salary. He also longed to return to Europe, especially Italy, and revisit those places he had seen during the war. Finally, he made an arrangement with the *Toronto Star*. He would send free-lance dispatches to the paper from all over Europe; in return he would be paid both for his articles and for expenses involved in getting the stories. In the fall of 1921, he and Hadley left their apartment in Chicago and headed for Europe. Their plan was to live on the Left Bank in Paris, where the cost of living was cheap, and the company the best. Sherwood Anderson had given Ernest letters of introduction to some of the foremost literary people of the day. It was an ideal arrangement for a young writer-to-be.

Ernest liked Paris very much, and enjoyed the life of a young expatriate. The city was full of young writers and artists, who felt, as he did, that America was not a very good environment for becoming a good writer. He made some very valuable literary acquaintances there. Among them were Gertrude Stein, who taught him a great deal; Ezra Pound, who became one of his best friends; Sylvia Beach, who owned a bookstore called Shakespeare and Co., and gained literary fame by publishing James Joyce's *Ulysses;* and Ford Madox Ford, with whom Ernest later worked on a little magazine called the *transatlantic review,* and who had been a friend of Joseph Conrad's. There were many others, of course, some of whom managed to gain literary recognition, and others who were just pretentious. Both types interested Ernest, and they were to become the source of his first novel, *The Sun Also Rises*.

Ernest learned a lot about politics in Europe, as well. His job as a correspondent took him to many places and introduced him to all levels of society. He also learned much from other correspondents. He wrote articles on a wide range of subjects. He covered the Genoa Economic Conference in 1922, and saw some bloody street encounters between Fascists and Communists. Later in the same year, he went to Constantinople to cover the war between Greece and Turkey. And, in 1923, he saw his first bullfight in Spain, an event which fascinated him. He began to pursue this sport as he had boxing in the past--not satisfied just to be a spectator, but having to get involved.

Being a correspondent, however, was but a means to an end for Hemingway: he was working very hard to become a writer. Through Ezra Pound, he met Robert McAlmon, a publisher, with whom he had arranged to publish his first book. It was to consist of short stories and poetry, and to be called, appropriately, *Three Stories and Ten Poems.* This arrangement was made in March, 1923, and Ernest had to work quickly on the book; Hadley was now pregnant, and both Ernest and Hadley thought it would be best for the child if he were born either in the United States or Canada. In

July, the book was finished, and they returned to Toronto. Ernest's stay there was not an especially good one; he did not get along with the new managing editor of the *Star*. His plans were to return to Europe as soon as the baby was born, for Toronto was not literary enough to suit him anymore. He worked hard to get some reviewer to look at his new book, and also worked on a volume of short stories that he intended to bring out next. Edmund Wilson read his book, and wrote him a letter, suggesting that he give up poetry and stick to prose: it was good advice, and Ernest followed it.

On October 10, 1923, Ernest's first son, John Hadley Nicanor Hemingway, was born ("Nicanor" after one of Ernest's favorite bullfighters); but he would go by the nickname "Bumby." The birth of the new baby, and Ernest's impending resignation from the *Star*, forced the young couple to leave Toronto in January, 1924 without paying the rent on their apartment.

Back in Paris, Ernest took up with his old friends again. He did not have much money coming in, but he managed to live on very little, and continued his writing. He helped Ford Madox Ford with his little magazine, the *Transatlantic Review*, which earned him no pay, but did gain for him some recognition. The magazine reviewed *Three Stories and Ten Poems*, and also *In Our Time*, the book of short stories he had been working on (which was published in Paris in a limited edition by Bill Bird in the spring of 1924).

These first two books were an excellent beginning for the young writer. They established him in the genre that many critics consider to be his best, the short story. The stories in *Three Stories and Ten Poems* were all good: "Up in Michigan" was a sad story about a sexual encounter between two people in Michigan, told briefly and honestly; "My Old Man," a story about a jockey and his son, reminded many readers of the best of Sherwood Anderson's stories; the third was "Out of Season," set in Switzerland. *In Our Time* contained some of his very best short stories, several of them about Nick Adams, including "The Three-Day Blow", "Big Two-Hearted River" and "Indian Camp"; it also included "The Battler," an especially good story which showed off Hemingway's real talent for writing dialogue. Between the stories, Ernest included brief "sketches," which were no more than one or two paragraphs in length, and were generally about Nick's war experiences or about bullfighting. The stories were very compact and interesting, and were good illustrations of the young writer's idea that if the writer knew what he was talking about, not much had to be said to give the reader the whole picture.

He went to the bullfights again in 1924, as he had done the year before, and took a whole string of friends along with him, including John Dos Passos. This time, he participated himself in the amateur bullfights, much to the delight and horror of the crowd. Ernest couldn't get enough of bullfighting, and was soon to write the first of several moving tributes to it in his first novel. The violence and tragedy of the sport attracted him. He was fascinated with anything that smelled of death, perhaps because he was trying to understand it. He had deliberately pursued death in the past when he went to the front lines in Italy; and without a war to got to, he found the next best thing in bullfighting. As a writer, he found it important to get as close to death as possible without actually dying, so that he could write honestly about it.

Success was not far away by this time. There was a growing interest in his first two books. When *In Our Time* went out of print in the Paris edition, there was still enough demand for the book so that by the middle of 1925, an American publishing company, Boni and Liveright, decided to publish the book again. This company was Sherwood Anderson's publisher, and Anderson had had some influence in this matter. It was the second time that Ernest had received a boost from the older writer.

In the meantime Ernest had begun his first novel only to abandon it. Entitled *Along With Youth* had been intended to be about Nick Adams (who was Ernest Hemingway only slightly disguised) and his adventures during the first world war. The book began on the ship *Chicago* with Nick getting acquainted with those on board; but it progressed no further.

In the summer of 1925, Ernest went to his third season of bullfights in Spain, and it was no doubt during this trip that the ideas formed for the novel that he would start and finish. He began its writing while he was still in Spain, and much of what he wrote must have been almost simultaneous with the events actually happening. Several of the characters in the book had real-life counterparts: the novel's Lady Brett Ashley was a girl named Duff Twysden who was along with them; Robert Cohn was based upon a writer named Harold Loeb; and Jake Barnes was modeled from no less than Ernest Hemingway himself. Circumstances were changed a bit, but the similarities were far too clear to be merely accidental.

In the meantime, a young American writer named Scott Fitzgerald had read *In Our Time*, and liked it so much that he began to recommend the young writer, whom he had never met, to his own publisher, Scribner's. Fitzgerald came to Paris to meet Hemingway, and to try to persuade him to change publishers. Ernest liked Fitzgerald very well; and he liked the idea of working for Scribner's, but he was under contract to Boni and Liveright.

The proposal, however, led to a somewhat controversial episode in the young writer's career. For some time, he had been tired of having people compare his work with Sherwood Anderson's. Anderson had produced one very good book, *Winesburg, Ohio*, but his later work had left itself wide open to satire. As soon as Ernest finished the manuscript of his novel, *The Sun Also Rises*, he began immediately to work on another one, which would be a parody of Anderson's style. He knew that if he sent such a manuscript to Boni and Liveright, Anderson's publishers, they could hardly accept it and risk offending one of their best clients. This would leave Ernest free to send his novel to any publisher he wanted. It did not take him long to finish the parody, which he called *The Torrents of Spring*. As he showed it around to his friends, he received mixed reactions. Although some thought it was funny, almost everyone urged him not to publish it, because everyone liked Sherwood Anderson. Hadley thought it was terrible that he could insult such an old friend. But a friend of Hadley's Pauline Pfeiffer, was falling in love with Ernest, and she recommended that he go ahead and publish it. The book also angered Gertrude Stein: Part Four of *Torrents* was called "The Making and Marring of Americans," which sounded suspiciously like the title of one of her most famous books, *The Making of Americans*.

As expected, the manuscript was turned down by Boni and Liveright, leaving Ernest free to choose another publisher. On May 28, 1926, *The Torrents of Spring* was published by Scribner's, and on October 22, 1926, *The Sun Also Rises* was published. *Torrents* cost him a few friends, of course, but it also made him a few. Anderson did not like the book, but he was to prove an extremely generous individual, continuing to praise Hemingway's work in years to come; and indeed Hemingway was not the only writer to satirize him during those years. Hemingway's chief device in the book was to put his characters in improbable, but somehow mundane situations, and have them asking pretentious questions about the universe. It was just this kind of pretentiousness that Ernest found easy game for satire.

It was *The Sun Also Rises*, however, that projected Hemingway to the status of a major writer. It was a very good book, which attracted considerable critical and popular attention. The book was so good, in fact, that it is still considered by some people to be his best. It is about a group of expatriates living their sometimes-shocking (to Americans) lives in Paris in the twenties, and the things that happened to them during a summer in Spain in the bullfight season. The "hero" of the book is Jake Barnes, a writer, who is impotent because of a war wound. Jake tells the story. More importantly, however, it is about Lady Brett Ashley: a freedom-loving and high-spirited woman, able and willing to attract several lovers at a time, she is really in love with Jake, and he with her, but they cannot consummate their love because of his wound. Along on the trip to Spain are Jake, Mike Campbell (the man to whom Lady Brett is engaged), and

Robert Cohn, who also thinks he has a chance with her. Instead, she gives most of her attention to a bullfighter named Romero. The book had all the elements of good gossip about the "shameless" life in Paris, and for this reason it sold well. However, the lasting value that made it a really good book was the sadness that emerged through all the laughter and drunkenness-- and the idea that these characters, like all other mere mortals, were also doomed. Hemingway had made his characters seem very real. He had shown their faults, which were many, as well as their virtues. And he had captured the moods of Paris in the twenties, and of Spain during the fiesta. At the same time, without meaning to, he had popularized a phrase first coined by Gertrude Stein in reference to the expatriates: "the lost generation."

Yet while Hemingway's literary fortunes were rising in 1926, his personal life was not. He did not enjoy his fourth year at the bullfights as much as he would have liked, finding himself torn between his wife and another woman, Pauline Pfeiffer. He finally decided to divorce Hadley and to give her the royalties from *The Sun Also Rises*. Money for himself did not seem to concern him. He had rich friends, and Pauline had some wealthy relatives back in Piggot, Arkansas. His divorce became final in January of 1927, and he and Pauline were married in May.

He did manage to publish another book of short stories in October of that year, entitled *Men Without Women*, possibly the best collection of short stories that he ever wrote. It contained three stories that qualify as his very best. One was about an aging boxer, and was called "Fifty Grand." Another, "The Undefeated," was about an aging bullfighter. These two stories had similar themes: they were about men who did not give up, even in the face of sure defeat. A third story in *Men Without Women* may be his best: it was another Nick Adams story called "The Killers," and it tells about two killers from the city who visit a lunchroom where Nick happens to be eating. With much bullying and tough banter, they announce they are going to kill a fellow named Ole Anderson. Nick runs off to warn

Anderson, only to find that Anderson knows he cannot escape the killers and therefore decides to do nothing. This decision surprises Nick, and teaches him a valuable lesson about the world. This story (like many of the Nick Adams stories) shows a moment in the life of Nick when he is initiated into some new knowledge of how the world really is. It is very well written, especially the dialogue between the killers and the other people in the restaurant.

Hemingway's misfortunes, however, continued. In December, 1927, he nearly lost the sight in his good eye, when his son Bumby accidentally poked him. And in the spring of 1928, a skylight fell on his head, and he had to be rushed to a hospital for stitches. He was bothered with recurrent sore throats. All of these troubles interrupted a novel he was working on. He finally abandoned the novel, and began working on another one that would eventually become *A Farewell to Arms*. He also began making plans to return to America to live; Pauline was pregnant, and again he thought it best to have his children born in the U.S. They decided to try Key West, which had been recommended by a friend; their plan was to stay there for a few months, to see if they liked it, then go to Piggot to visit Pauline's relatives, and then decide where to have the baby. Ernest liked Key West at once. He found that he could write very well there, and he liked the fishing. He soon fell into the happy pattern that he would know for the next few years, visiting Sloppy Joe's Bar in his leisure time, and talking and drinking with all sorts of people who came in there. He liked fishing for big fish, and he liked talking to fishermen.

His parents, by coincidence, were in St. Petersburg. Ernest's father was thinking about buying some real estate in Florida. They came down for a visit with their son and their new daughter-in-law. It was a happy occasion, in spite of the fact that Dr. Hemingway and his wife had not approved of the divorce.

When it was time for the baby, Ernest drove Pauline to Kansas City, where she would have good medical care. The baby was born in Research Hospital on June 28, 1928. It was not an easy birth; a Caesarean section had to be performed. The baby was a boy, and they named him Patrick. Because of the operation, Pauline needed some time to recuperate; as soon as she and the baby could travel, he took them both back to Piggot, and then set off with an old friend for Wyoming, where he planned to get in a little fishing and hunting, and to work on his novel. Pauline joined him later, and after about another month, they returned to Key West. They had not been there long when word came that Ernest's father had committed suicide. Ernest received word of the death by telegraph in New York, where he had come to get Bumby for a visit to Key West. He sent Bumby on, took a train to Chicago, and moved in with his family for a few days where he soon learned the reasons for his father's suicide. Dr. Hemingway had come into a run of bad luck, both medical and financial. He had discovered that he had diabetes, and for some reason had no desire to take care of it. In addition, he had lost a lot of his savings in the Florida real estate deal. This could have put the family into economic difficulty, had not Ernest nearly finished his new novel, which made it possible for him to help out a little.

After the funeral he returned to Key West, taking his sister Sunny with him to help him finish the manuscript of *A Farewell to Arms*. It was finished in January, 1929, and sent off to the publisher. In April, Ernest went back to Europe, taking along his family (including Bumby and Sunny) to visit old friends and to go to the bullfights again in Spain.

A Farewell to Arms was published in September, just after the end of the bullfight season. Ernest passed it around to his friends in Europe and they all declared it to be very good. The critics agreed. The book received better reviews than any book he had ever written, and it was soon a bestseller. This was fortunate for Ernest, for it meant that he would not feel the sting of the Great Depression, which was on the way. In *A Farewell to Arms* Ernest drew upon his war experiences and his love affair with Agnes von Kurowsky. The novel told the story of Frederick Henry, who, like Hemingway, was a young ambulance driver during the war. Also like Hemingway, Henry is wounded and taken to a field hospital, where he meets a young nurse named Catherine Barkley. In the novel, the young soldier and the nurse fall in love, and she becomes pregnant. With the retreat from Caporetto, Frederick joins Catherine and they escape together to Switzerland in a boat: they make it alive, but Catherine then dies in childbirth. The description of the retreat was especially well written and is perhaps the chief reason why the book deserved so much praise.

In January, 1930, Hemingway returned to Key West, and began to make plans for a safari to Africa. The idea had been building inside him for some time. It was to be a few years before he would actually go, but the idea had become definite. Meanwhile, many plans kept him busy. He was planning a big book on bullfighting, nonfiction with beautiful pictures, another long-term plan. That summer he went back to Wyoming for some more hunting and fishing. He liked the West very much, and he especially liked living on dude ranches. In August, 1930, he had another accident: a horse he was riding panicked and carried him into a woods where he was cut up enough to require stitches. It was not long until he had another accident: in November he was driving with some friends through Montana, when he was forced off the road and had a wreck. He broke his arm very badly and had to be hospitalized. In 1931, he returned to Key West for more fishing, and nursed his arm back to health. In April Pauline was pregnant again, and he began to make plans to go to Spain for the bullfights and to work on his book, so that they could return in the fall to have the baby in Kansas City as before. This was his seventh season of bullfights in nine years, and he came very close to completing his bullfight book. His third child, another Caesarean, was a boy, Gregory Hancock, born on November 12, 1931. In December, he went hunting in Piggot, and finished his book, which he called *Death in the Afternoon*.

In 1932 Hemingway bought a house in Key West. In April of that year he went fishing in Havana, and made one of the great discoveries of his life: marlin fishing.

But by the time *Death in the Afternoon* came out in the fall, he was back in Wyoming, hunting again, and putting together a new volume of short stories.

Reviews of *Death in the Afternoon* were somewhat disappointing. Many people could not understand Hemingway's passionate interest in bullfighting; many found it too morbid to read. Perhaps the initial disappointment with the book was to severe; although later opinions have tended to agree that it was not as good as his earlier works, it was very good in its own way. It was undeniably a fine tribute to the sport and remains a favorite even of bullfighters on the subject.

In November, 1932 Ernest saw the film version of *A Farewell to Arms*. Although it did not please him, he did like the profit he had made from it. He returned to Key West in 1933, worked on his short stories, visited New York, returned, fished, worked on his stories some more, and went down to Havana, where he began writing articles, about fishing among other things, for *Esquire*, a new magazine published by Arnold Gingrich, a friend of his. He finished his book of short stories, calling it *Winner Take Nothing*. One of the stories in the book was the highly respected "A Clean, Well-Lighted Place," which was devotedly championed by some critics. Another was a startling story called "The Light of the World," which rivaled some of his best for dialogue.

With this book behind him, he was at last ready for his long-postponed safari. In August, 1933 Ernest and Pauline sailed for Spain, where they visited awhile and went, of course, to the bullfights. Then they went to Paris, where Ernest finished a short story about a Cuban fisherman and rum-runner named Harry Morgan, which would later develop into a novel called *To Have and Have Not*. From Paris, they went down to Africa by boat in November, and the safari began. The hunting went very well for awhile in December. But soon Ernest had developed a disease called amoebic dysentery, which gave him a fever and caused him to hemorrhage. Determined not to let this spoil his fun, he kept on hunting when he should have rested; he finally collapsed, and had to be flown to Nairobi for treatment. Flying in the plane to Nairobi, he saw Mt. Kilimanjaro, which looked very beautiful covered with snow, and it gave him the idea for a short story, "*The Snows of Kilimanjaro,*" one of his best. And he was soon back on his feet again, hunting all of those wild animals that he had dreamed about for so many years.

Ernest returned to Key West in April, 1934 and bought a fishing boat, naming it the *Pilar*. He spent the rest of the year getting used to the new boat, hunting marlin in Havana, and working on the manuscript of his new book, which was to be about his safari. When he finally got around, a year later, to going to Bimini in the *Pilar*, he had another of his strange accidents. On their way out, Ernest caught a shark, and pulled it up on the boat. He pulled out his pistol and began to shoot it; but the fish slipped and a bullet missed and richocheted into both of his legs. They had to return home, where he recuperated for about a week before they could start out again.

In August, 1935, a hurricane ripped through Key West. Although it did little damage to his boat or house, there was much devastation, and among the many dead bodies were some of his best friends. In October he went to New York for the publication of his safari book, which he called *The Green Hills of Africa*. Although the book was not fiction, it read very much as if it were. Ernest's idea, he said, was to write something that was absolutely true and see if it could compete with a work of fiction. It was a good hunting book, giving much practical information not only about hunting but about the ethics of hunting in Africa. The book received mixed reviews. As with *Death in the Afternoon*, few literary people were interested in the subject. This did not overly concern Ernest, though he was concerned a great deal about his literary status. Remembering the cool initial reception of *Death in the Afternoon*, and the steady praise it had received since then, he thought that the same would probably be true of *Green Hills*. And, as it turned out, he was right.

He wrote a second Harry Morgan story in December, 1935, and continued writing other stories throughout 1936. In August, he published the first of two very good African stories, *The Snows of Kilimanjaro,*" in *Esquire*. Obviously based on Hemingway's own experience, it was the story of a writer named Harry, who goes on safari in the hope that the experience will give him many important things to write about. But he develops gangrene before he can finish his adventure, and realizes that before the rescue plane can get to him, he will probably die. In a dream, just before he dies, a plane comes and carries him over Mt. Kilimanjaro.

The other story was "The Short Happy Life of Francis Macomber," published in October in *Cosmopolitan*. In this story, Francis Macomber is on safari, and has proven himself to be a coward by running from a lion he has wounded. He is saved by his guide, but his wife begins to ridicule him. Later, he wounds a buffalo, and his cowardice vanishes as he follows it into the trees. When the buffalo charges, he is ready; his wife shoots at the buffalo, missing, and killing Francis.

The Spanish Civil War had begun in July of 1936. In November, back in Key West, he decided to go to Spain to cover the war as a correspondent. Before leaving, however, he planned to finish the manuscript of the new novel which had grown out of the Harry Morgan stories.

In December, while standing in Sloppy Joe's Bar in Key West, he met a young girl from St. Louis named Martha Gellhorn. Martha was a correspondent and novelist herself, and she and Ernest were immediately drawn to each other. She had come to Key West as a tourist with her family, and it wasn't long before she became a frequent guest of the Hemingways.

This meeting would eventually lead to the end of Ernest's second marriage and the beginning of his third.

In January, 1937, Hemingway was ready to go to Spain. He was first in Madrid, for about six months. Martha soon joined him there, as a correspondent for *Colliers*. Their relationship at this point was still just friendly, but Ernest had apparently been having problems at home.

The war was important to Hemingway for several reasons. He saw it as a trial run for Fascism in Europe, and he believed, rightly, that unless the Communist forces in Spain could win, there would be a much bigger war later on. During this first trip, he worked on a documentary film called *The Spanish Earth,* which he intended to use to raise funds for ambulances during the war. He left Spain in May, and returned to New York and Key West, giving propaganda speeches on behalf of the Spanish people, and showing his film. Martha managed to get a White House showing for it, and both President and Mrs. Roosevelt thought it was very good, and agreed with the sentiments expressed. He also showed it in Hollywood, where he was able to raise considerable funds.

He went back to Spain in August, where Martha soon joined him. She and Ernest were becoming very close by this time. It was she who had arranged the White House showing of his film, and she was becoming his strongest champion. Pauline, in contrast, could not understand why he needed to get so involved with this particular war.

In October the Harry Morgan novel was published, under the title *To Have and Have Not.* It was more a collection of a few long stories than a novel, but the stories were closely related in subject matter. In the book, Harry Morgan is the ill-fated owner of a fishing boat during the depression. Plagued by bad luck, he sometimes has to make a living by illegal means, smuggling everything from people to liquor. On one of these trips, he is shot, and loses an arm. On another, he is forced to kill one man to save the lives of several others. And, finally, he is killed himself, aiding some bank robbers.

Reviews of the book were mixed. The first section of the book was very good: Ernest had written a rather long story in such a way that it seemed very short. The remainder of the book, however, seemed hurried and unfinished; some critics called it episodic. Others, however, noted what they considered a good turn in Hemingway's works. They discerned (or so they thought) a new interest in politics: this pleased many critics of the New Left, which was becoming very popular in those days. Harry Morgan was certainly a victim, it seemed, of an ignorant government. And at one point in the novel, he declared that one man, alone, hasn't got a chance in the world. This seemed a bit different from the existential independence of Hemingway's earlier novels. Despite critical reservations, however, there was one gratifying result from the publication of the novel: it became a best-seller.

By the time that *To Have and Have Not* was published, Ernest was already working on a play based on the Spanish Civil War, called *The Fifth Column*. Pauline, curious about Ernest's affairs, came to Spain in December, 1937, to see what was going on, and returned with him to the United States in January, 1938. This was not a happy time for Ernest. He was disturbed by the slow progress of the war, by bad reviews of his works, by guilt over his affair with Martha, and by physical problems which included liver trouble.

In the fall, his play appeared, along with a group of short stories, under the title *The Fifth Column and the First Forty-Nine Stories*. As with so many of his other books in the past, reviews were mixed. The play did, however, popularize the term "fifth column" (enemy sympathizers within a city, who could do much damage during a war).

By 1939, Hemingway was seeing less and less of his wife, and more and more of Martha. In February he went to Cuba, where he began working on his Spanish Civil War novel. Martha soon joined him there. By September of that year, Ernest and Pauline had agreed to separate, and Ernest took Martha to Sun Valley. There, he went hunting and fishing and worked on his novel, which by this time was beginning to bore Martha. She went off to Finland late that year, to cover the war that had developed there, returning to Cuba in January, 1940, to find Ernest still working hard on his novel. Finally in July he had the manuscript completed.

He was very pleased with the results. He knew it was his best book in years. Published in October, 1940 under the title *For Whom the Bell Tolls*, and it was his first novel in years to win almost unanimous praise. It was a long book, longer than his others, and it told about the guerrillas in the hills in Spain who fought for the Communist cause without questioning its merits. The hero of the book is an American, who, of course, resembles Hemingway in many ways, and whose assignment is to join the guerrillas and blow up a bridge. In doing so, he becomes involved with a pretty girl named Maria; a strong-willed old woman named Pilar; her husband Pablo, a once-brave and now cowardly fighter; a deaf but determined guerrilla leader named El Sordo; and a very sturdy old man named Anselmo. There are many moving and frightening scenes in the novel, including Pilar's account of the killing, one by one, of several Fascist leaders in a small town, and the account of El Sordo's last stand on a hillside with a handful of gypsies against a Fascist cavalry and airplane assault. The book was such a huge success that it was soon made into a very popular movie, starring Gary Cooper and Ingrid Bergman.

The success of *For Whom the Bell Tolls* was heartening, and it was to be the last novel that Hemingway would publish in nearly ten years. His divorce from Pauline became official in November, 1940, and he was soon married to Martha in Wyoming. In 1941, the "new" couple went to China, to inspect the war that was developing there between China and Japan. Since he was a celebrity whose knowledge of military tactics was respected, Hemingway was entertained by Chiang Kai-shek, and taken to the front lines. He returned to the United States predicting, rightly, that America would soon be at war, and that the attack from the enemy could begin in the Pacific. He returned to Havana for a while, then went to Sun Valley, and was driving through Texas when the news of the bombing of Pearl Harbor came over the radio in December.

In 1942, Ernest did not do a great deal of writing, nor did he show any inclination to go to the war, though Martha tried to persuade him to.

In May, he came up with one of his more original ideas, which he presented to the American ambassador. His idea was to take the *Pilar* and stock it with ammunition. He would then cruise around Cuba and the southern part of Florida, pretending to be on a scientific expedition, trying to attract the attention of any German submarines that might be in the area. If such a submarine were to surface and question them, the plan was then to shoot everyone on deck and try to drop a bomb down the hatch. It was an interesting idea, and since it was Hemingway who asked to do it, he managed to get permission. He did not, however, have any luck, though the radio on the *Pilar* did confirm that German submarines were in the area.

By the end of 1943, Martha had gone off to the war as a correspondent for *Collier's,* and Ernest followed her in 1944, getting a job as chief correspondent for the same magazine, which made him Martha's boss. In March he was in London, waiting for the invasion of England. There he met Mary Welsh, another correspondent, who was working for *Time, Life,* and *Fortune* at the time. He had another of his many accidents while he was there. He was riding through the streets of London one night during a blackout, returning from a party, when the car he was riding in hit a steel water tank. Ernest's head had rammed into the windshield, and he was hurt badly enough to be taken to a hospital. Martha came to see him, but, disapproving of his activities, she did not offer much sympathy. It was during this period that the conflict between these two strong personalities began to grow, and Ernest began to devote his attentions more to Mary Welsh.

As might be expected, Ernest was not satisfied just to report the war; he had to get involved as well. By May of 1944 he was out of the hospital, defying doctors' orders not to drink or fly. He saw the D-Day invasion, flew on missions with the Royal Air Force, followed the front into France, saw the liberation of Paris, and went into Germany. All this time, he was suffering from headaches brought on by the car accident and previous injuries.

In March, 1945, he returned to Havana, where he went fishing, and spent a great deal of time restoring his villa, Finca Vigia. In December, 1945, he officially divorced Martha, and in March, 1946, he married Mary Welsh in Havana.

The years between 1946 and 1950, were times of frustration and interruption. Hemingway began work on one novel, *The Garden of Eden,* only to abandon it. He began and finished another, called *Across the River and Into the Trees*. Mary nearly died once. (Ernest was luckily on hand to save her life). His two sons by Pauline (Patrick and Gregory) were in an automobile wreck. His good friend and publisher Max Perkins died. His lawyer died. On a trip to Europe in 1949, Mary broke her ankle in a skiing accident, and Ernest became very ill with an eye infection. *Across the River and Into the Trees* was published in September, 1950, and it was the low point in his literary career. Very few reviewers had any praise for the book. The publication of such an unsuccessful book, after his having produced none in ten years, indicated to many people that Hemingway was finished as a writer.

The reading public, however, had given up on Hemingway too soon. He was working on several novels about the sea, and in 1951 he found himself writing with great ease and quality. He wrote the story of an old fisherman named Santiago, who had not had a catch for many months, and who goes out one day and catches the biggest marlin of his life. The book was to be, apparently, part of a series which would make up a longer book, but in 1952 Ernest decided to publish it separately under the title *The Old Man and the Sea*. It was first published in *Life* magazine in September and a week later by Scribner's. The response to this book was as good as the response to his previous book had been bad. It was a very good book, said the critics, possibly the best he had ever written. The struggle with the fish had seemed sad and brutal but natural, they said, and Hemingway had approached his best theme, the struggle of aging men against unbeatable odds, in the best way possible. Santiago knew, long before he got home with his fish, that the sharks would have it eaten, but he struggled on anyway. And there was a feeling approaching love in the old man for the fish he had caught, for the fish had struggled nobly for its life. This strong relationship between the old man and nature gave Santiago a kind of spiritual quality that other Hemingway heroes lacked. This was the last book that Hemingway was to publish while he was alive, and it was a fine finish to almost three decades of writing and publishing fiction.

His life was far from over, however. He continued to live as he had always lived. He worked on several books in his last years, and he hunted and fished whenever possible. He went to Spain and France and back to Africa for a second safari, nearly dying in two plane crashes there.

Hemingway won both the Pulitzer Prize and the Nobel Prize for literature.

In 1955, he worked with Spencer Tracy on the film version of *The Old Man and the Sea*. He went to the bullfights, writing articles about his favorite bullfighters. He went hunting in Wyoming. He went to Sun Valley, and had a house in Ketchum, Idaho.

Hemingway probably would have continued to live in Cuba, if conditions had remained stable in that country. When America began to have its problems with Castro, however, he decided to quietly leave the Finca Vigia, and moved to Idaho.

In 1960, his health failing, he was in and out of the Mayo Clinic. He lost weight, his blood pressure went up, and he was having trouble with his kidneys. In addition to all of these problems, he was finding it very difficult to write. He became depressed.

In late June, 1961, he was ready to return to Ketchum from his last stay at the clinic. Upon his release, Mary asked a friend to drive them back to Idaho. It was not an especially pleasant trip: Ernest did not seem to be himself. He seemed very concerned about getting back, and checked the maps all the time, asking where they were. When they finally arrived, he seemed a bit relieved and perked up a bit; however his depression returned. On the morning of July 2, 1962, rising early, he went to the basement and took out a favorite shotgun; setting it on the floor, he shot himself in the head with both barrels.

In his life, as he remains in the legend, Ernest Hemingway was as popular as any politician, sports figure or movie star. Perhaps this was because he was a little of all three or more. Perhaps it was because his life-style, his preoccupation with courage, was a symbol of how to live. Nothing could kill him, he seemed to insist. He had to do that himself.

BIBLIOGRAPHY

I. BOOKS BY HEMINGWAY:

The following titles are available from various publishers. Here they are listed with the date of their original publication.

Across the River and Into the Trees, a novel (1950)
By-Line, newspaper and magazine articles (1967)
Death In the Afternoon, non-fiction (1932)
A Farewell to Arms, a novel (1929)
The Fifth Column, a play (1938)
For Whom the Bell Tolls, a novel (1940)
The Green Hills of Africa, non-fiction (1935)
In Our Time, short stories (1924)
Islands in the Stream, a novel (1970)
Men Without Women, short stories (1927)
A Moveable Feast, non-fiction (1964)
The Nick Adams Stories, short stories (1972)
The Old Man and the Sea, a novelette (1952)
The Sun Also Rises, a novel (1926)
To Have and Have Not, a novel (1937)
The Torrents of Spring, a satirical novel (1926)
Winner Take Nothing, short stories (1933)

II. BOOKS ABOUT HEMINGWAY'S LIFE:

Baker, Carlos. *Ernest Hemingway; a Life Story*. New York, Scribners, 1969.

Callaghan, Morley. *That Summer in Paris; Memories of Tangled Friendships with Hemingway, Fitzgerald, and some Others*. New York, Coward-McCann, 1963.

Hemingway, Leicester. *My Brother, Ernest Hemingway*. Cleveland World Publishing Company, 1962.

Hotchner, A. E. *Papa Hemingway; a Personal Memoir*. New York, Random House, 1966.

Kiley, John. *Hemingway: An Old Friend Remembers*. New York, Hawthorn Books, 1965.

Sanford, Marcelline (Hemingway). *At the Hemingways; a Family Portrait*. Boston, Little, Brown, 1962.

Seward, William. *My Friend, Ernest Hemingway; an Affectionate Reminiscence*. South Brunswick, A. S. Barnes, 1969.

III. BOOKS OF CRITICISM ABOUT HEMINGWAY'S WORKS:

Baker, Carlos. *Ernest Hemingway: Critiques of Four Major Novels.* New York, Scribner's, 1962.

Baker, Sheridan. *Ernest Hemingway; an Introduction and Interpretation.* New York, Holt, Rinehart, and Winston, 1967.

Killinger, John. *Hemingway and the Dead Gods: a Study in Existentialism.* Lexington, University of Kentucky Press, 1960.

McCaffery, John. *Ernest Hemingway: the Man and his Work.* New York, Cooper Square Publishers, 1969.

Ross, Lillian. *Portrait of Hemingway.* New York, Simon and Schuster, 1961.

Rovitt, Earl. *Ernest Hemingway.* New York, Twayne Publishers, 1963.

White, William. *The Merrill Checklist of Ernest Hemingway.* Columbus, Ohio, Merrill, 1970.

Weeks, Robert. *Hemingway; a Collection of Critical Essays.* Englewood Cliffs, New Jersey, Prentice-Hall, 1962.

Young, Phillip. *The Hemingway Manuscripts; an Inventory.* University Park, Pennsylvania, State University Press, 1969.

SamHar Press
Division of Story House Corp.